MIX
Papier aus verantwortungsvollen Quellen
Paper from responsible sources
FSC® C105338

Ginika Egesimba

RSM2

Anchor Compact

Egesimba, Ginika: RSM2. Hamburg, Anchor Academic Publishing 2014

Buch-ISBN: 978-3-95489-265-5
PDF-eBook-ISBN: 978-3-95489-765-0
Druck/Herstellung: Anchor Academic Publishing, Hamburg, 2014

Bibliografische Information der Deutschen Nationalbibliothek:
Die Deutsche Nationalbibliothek verzeichnet diese Publikation in der Deutschen Nationalbibliografie; detaillierte bibliografische Daten sind im Internet über http://dnb.d-nb.de abrufbar

Bibliographical Information of the German National Library:
The German National Library lists this publication in the German National Bibliography. Detailed bibliographic data can be found at: http://dnb.d-nb.de

All rights reserved. This publication may not be reproduced, stored in a retrieval system or transmitted, in any form or by any means, electronic, mechanical, photocopying, recording or otherwise, without the prior permission of the publishers.

Das Werk einschließlich aller seiner Teile ist urheberrechtlich geschützt. Jede Verwertung außerhalb der Grenzen des Urheberrechtsgesetzes ist ohne Zustimmung des Verlages unzulässig und strafbar. Dies gilt insbesondere für Vervielfältigungen, Übersetzungen, Mikroverfilmungen und die Einspeicherung und Bearbeitung in elektronischen Systemen.

Die Wiedergabe von Gebrauchsnamen, Handelsnamen, Warenbezeichnungen usw. in diesem Werk berechtigt auch ohne besondere Kennzeichnung nicht zu der Annahme, dass solche Namen im Sinne der Warenzeichen- und Markenschutz-Gesetzgebung als frei zu betrachten wären und daher von jedermann benutzt werden dürften.

Die Informationen in diesem Werk wurden mit Sorgfalt erarbeitet. Dennoch können Fehler nicht vollständig ausgeschlossen werden und die Diplomica Verlag GmbH, die Autoren oder Übersetzer übernehmen keine juristische Verantwortung oder irgendeine Haftung für evtl. verbliebene fehlerhafte Angaben und deren Folgen.

Alle Rechte vorbehalten

© Anchor Academic Publishing, ein Imprint der Diplomica® Verlag GmbH
http://www.diplom.de, Hamburg 2014
Printed in Germany

Content

Content 1

Abstract 3

The Comparative Impact of Globalization of Clinical Trials in India and China 5

Indian drug regulatory body versus the Chinese system 7

Ethics in Indian drug development versus Chinese; global clinical trial impact 12

Evolution of Indian ICH-GCP and the Chinese ICH-GCP processes 16

Intellectual property protection, government role and involvement in research 19

Abstract

India and China have been identified by pharmaceutical companies as the future markets that would support drug research and development in a cost efficient manner. This has become necessary as resources to conduct clinical studies dwindle, coupled with the fact that pharmaceutical industries are under pressure to deliver quality medicine, on time, to the public. Exploring and examining India and China's potential in a stepwise fashion provides the opportunity to dissect the good, the bad and the ugly of globalization in a comparative approach. This paper will cover areas like ethics in the conduct of studies, good clinical practice (GCP), economic realities, ICH influence, intellectual property security and the role of government in global clinical trial.

The Comparative Impact of Globalization of Clinical Trials in India and China

Increasingly, resources for conducting clinical trials continue to dwindle following pressure from other economic competing priorities. To this end, pharmaceutical industries look for more innovative ways of delivering medicinal products to the door steps of end users who are in need of quality medicines for their health. In addition, pharmaceutical industries are also faced with the challenge of a more cost efficient way of doing business which culminates to balancing quality, time and cost (Phillips, 2005). The outcome of this development is the exploration of off-shore drug research and development. This is also referred to as outsourcing of clinical trials, as well as globalization of clinical studies.

India and China have been identified as potential hubs and are currently being explored by large and medium scale pharmaceutical/biotechnology companies as future markets. These two countries hold great potentials, considering the abundance of humans in need of quality medicine, the labor workforce with Western education to support clinical studies at a reduced cost, upcoming infrastructures that are of internationally recognized standards, a mixture of relaxed and complex regulatory pathways and drug naïve subjects that are ready to enroll in trials. These two emerging markets are also in the process of aligning their regulatory guidelines and laws with that of the Western world. As rosy as this appears, there are still hurdles to overcome in these countries being explored by pharmaceutical industries.

Some large pharma industries, in trying to make the best of these opportunities, have entered into strategic alliances, collaboration and partnership with local industries and other multi-national CROs with the ability to navigate complex drug regulatory pathway to fast track business development and to conduct research (EMERGING MARKETS). However, this also comes with its attendant challenging risk of losing intellectual property, quality standard compromise and recruiting patients without consent (EMERGING MARKETS).

The speeds at which pharmaceutical industries are exploring these offshore terrains vary because of the competitive advantage of one region over the other or rather the way these countries are repositioning themselves to attract the capital market of the industry. This paper will explore and examine the good, the bad and the ugly in a comparative manner that has resulted following globalization of clinical trials. As the paper examines the impact of globalization, it will compare a broad range of globalization impacts on regulatory climates; ethics in the conduct of clinical trials; ICH influences (good clinical practice (GCP) and global acceptance including adaptation; intellectual property security; and the role of government in global clinical trials; economic realities.

Indian drug regulatory body versus the Chinese system

The increasing outsourcing of clinical trials to India stems from the fact that large pharmaceutical companies are pressured to deliver quality medicines to meet unmet needs in the society. In addition, dwindling research funds calls for more effective ways of doing business across the globe.

Not only that, companies are also interested in repositioning themselves to capture emerging markets as projection have shown that these markets hold great potentials for global clinical trials. The Indian pharmaceutical market capitalization was projected to grow to 2 billion US dollars as of 2010 (Chatterjee, 2008). India is now one of the emerging hubs for clinical trials as it boasts of technically competent and young workforce (More than 500,000 trained in the US and in the UK), low cost of drug development, availability of treatment naïve population, concentration of large population in urban cities, presence of major diseases, use of English as a means of communication, supportive infrastructure, population diversity, highest number of FDA-approved labs as well as friendly drug control systems (Chatterjee, 2008; Mukesh, 2009; Jankosky, Jiang,& Farwell, 2007 and China).

As companies try to take advantage of the potential gains presented by the outsourcing of clinical trials to emerging markets, their actions and inactions have impacted both positively and negatively in the evolutions of drug regulatory system, including uncovering gaps that have exposed patients to harm during trial conducts. Before now, India has demonstrated expertise in conducting research in generic medicines while hosting only 1% of US sponsored investigational new drug research (Mukesh, 2009). However, with increased outsourcing of clinical trials, and expected rise of FDA regulated drug research, India conducted 10% of FDA regulated studies back in 2010 and 15% in 2011 respectively (Jankosky,Jiang,& Farwell, 2007; Deepakmb, 2011). The Indian regulatory framework is repositioning itself and as well aligning its practices and organization to measure up to that of the West in order to make it competitive among emerging markets.

The Drug Controller General India (DCGI) has being restructured to serves as the Indian equivalent of Food and Drug Administration of the US and European Medicine agency in Europe. It is the Federal body regulating all pharmaceutical related issues in India as described in the drug and cosmetic rule of 2005 (Mukesh, 2009). The DCGI is equivalent to the FDA commissioner, while clinical trial is regulated per schedule Y of the drug and cosmetic rule, synonymous with the investigational new drug regulation described in 21 CFR 312 of the United States (Mukesh, 2009). This resemblance on the surface is attractive to Western countries as it makes India a favorable hub for clinical trials. The FDA is subdivided into various offices that address issues regarding new chemical entities, biologics and medical devices with designate leads. This is not the case with the DCGI, making regulatory approval cumbersome and complex. Drug approval in India could take as long as six months. Trial documents with queries may stay longer including trials considered as sensitive. Indian drug regulatory system was realigned to capture lead drug markets in 2006 by categorizing application in A&B. Category A are trials that have received approval in major markets (US, UK, Germany, South Africa, Canada, Australia and New Zealand including Europe) following the rigor and expertise of regulatory system in these countries. Proposal and protocol documents submitted under category A are given preference and reviewed within 2 - 4 weeks. The category B research is reviewed within 5 - 6 months (Mukesh, 2009). Before 2005, retesting of foreign drugs is required and in addition, the Indian regulatory system requires all research to be conducted in India to lag by one phase from the country outsourcing the trials (Deepakmb, 2011). However this has changed as parallel studies are now allowed making Indian suitable to participate in multinational trials.

As good and appealing as these prospects to clinical trial conduct, continual outsourcing of clinical studies to India has revealed that the gains of global clinical trial is that of a slow yet consistent improvement. The human resource for health needs of DCGI is yet to be addressed as the DCGI is only one person supported by a deputy that reviews research proposal documents submitted for research conduct. This has further lengthened research approval process to 6 - 8 weeks. There are still gaps in the tracking system for submitted files making it difficult for sponsor companies to accurately predict the position of submitted files and their status. In additions, global outsourcing to India is yet to address formal meetings with regulatory bodies before submission of files making it challenging in putting documents together to meet regulatory requirements (Mukesh, 2009).

China as an emerging market in Asia Pacific and as well a potential hub for the conduct of clinical trial across the globe features some unique advantages that make it attractive to lead markets in the pharmaceutical industries. Some of the potential it shares with India and beyond include; having the largest urban treatment naïve population, supportive and motivated workforce (18,000 hospitals, 1.5 million physicians, 2 million physician assistance, and 1.6 million nurses), significantly reduced cost of research conduct, abound and unique disease resources, a huge market, GCP compliant database and certified GCP public hospitals for research conduct. (Jankosky, Jiang, & Farwell, 2007; How to conduct clinical trials in china). To this end, it is expected that china will be the 3rd largest pharmaceutical market by 2020. Global clinical trials have impacted positively on the Chinese drug regulatory process to support clinical trials in this region.

China has already developed traditional research and development processes and systems. However, the quest for modern pharmaceutical remains obvious following the shifting dynamics of the Chinese population as well as the rapid urbanization of rural China (Emerging Market; Faiz & Eric, 2007). Beyond having a traditional medicine system, the Chinese government in a bid to reposition itself to become attractive to Western countries introduced her GCP in 1998. This version of the GCP was revised in 2003 by the Chinese State Food and Drug Administration- an equivalent of the US FDA created in 2000. A new drug administration law was also introduced in 2001 coupled with a new drug registration procedure in 2002 (How to conduct clinical trial in China) .Another impact seen with globalization of clinical studies in the Chinese system was the adoption of the World Trade Organization recommendation on patent law protection and intellectual property right in 2002. To make her shores competitive and attractive for innovative drug investigation, the regulatory system has extended patent law and intellectual property rights to 20 years.

Far above the introduction of drug regulatory process and new procedures for the registration of drugs in the early 2000, China lately streamlined its drug regulatory processes coordinated by the Chinese State Food and Drug Administration (SFDA). Some of these changes include the conduct of clinical trials by only GCP-certified sites, the presence of US FDA offices in China, strict monitoring of sites where trials are ongoing, shortening of drug approval processes making (90 working days in 2007), the centralization of the drug regulatory processes and harmonization of multicenter clinical trial conduct in 2007 including the inclusion of international trials in Chinese regulation for the first time

(How to conduct clinical trials in China; Jurij &Petrin). The Chinese population dynamic shift that contributes to China's competitive advantage in clinical trial conduct is uncovering the participation of increasing number of aged population in clinical studies. This is a grey area which increasing outsourcing of clinical studies to China will explore. Global outsourcing in this region will address research in elderly including the care of aged population across the globe. This is likely going to be one of the impacts of and revelations of global clinical trial outsourcing.

Ethics in Indian drug development versus Chinese; global clinical trial impact

The need for good and improved medicines stands out as one of the compelling reasons for the move of clinical trials to emerging markets. Testing drug in human before approval is a pre-requisite, however this requires extreme care as these markets offer a large population of treatment naïve and vulnerable patients with diversity of diseases and gene variability, to support drug studies (Deepakmb, 2011). In addition, weak and poorly constituted ethic committee in emerging markets has provided the platform for exploiting vulnerable populations.

Following outsourcing of clinical trials in India, havoc, horror, and harm have been witnessed and recorded during clinical trial conducts. Ethic committees in India are saddled with clinical trial document (Protocol, informed consent form, protocol amendment risk assessment etcetera) review and as well support the DCGI when consulted to review submitted document by foreign sponsors (Deepakmb, 2011). These ethic committees however are not under the control of the DCGI nor accountable to any public authority.

There is also no formal registration of the ethic review committees in India. The number of existing ethic committee cannot be estimated nor registration with regulatory body required before they commence operation. In addition, private medical centers conduct research involving human without adequate consultations with regulatory bodies (Mukesh, 2009). Most of these ethic committees are staffed with physicians working in institutions where the research is being conducted (Mukesh, 2009). Fewer than 40 ethic committees in Indian are well constituted, making safety of Indian subjects of great concern (Mukesh, 2009; Deepakmb, 2011 ; Clinical trial ethics in Indian one step forward two steps backwards) The resultant effect is the loss of focus of her (ethic committee) core responsibility of protecting human subjects of research. The ultimate effect is comprises in research document review (informed consent document, risk benefit analysis and research protocol), poor monitoring of ongoing trial and lack of accountability in the form of progress notes. The delinking of the DCGI as the legal regulator from the ethical regulators (ethic committees) has demonstrated the inefficiency in the system. These gaps have introduced questionable and unethical research practices.

Reports of recent misconduct in public and private health sector in India on mentally challenged persons over a period of 2 years (2008-2010) put to question the functionality of the ethic committees in these institutions including their understanding of the principles of respect for person, beneficence and justice (Clinical trial ethics in Indian one step forward two steps backwards). In the past three years (2010-2013), 1,542 deaths have been recorded in India resulting from participation in research. 668 occurred in 2010 with drug companies admitting that only 22 are directly related to their trials (Serious adverse events). 438 and 436 occurred in 2011 respectively. 211 were admitted to be drug related injury in 2012.

The fact that compensation is yet to be paid to more than 85% of families of subjects affected in line with GCP requirements continue to buttress the gaps in ethical regulation of Indian clinical trials. (The Tribune, February 23, 2013).

With increasing outsourcing of clinical studies, the Indian regulatory system is also undergoing critical reforms to forestall human subject injuries during research proceedings. One such reform is the push for the centralization of drug regulatory systems. In 2008, the Indian counsel of medical research and reputable journals have also called for the mandatory clinical trial registration in the Indian clinical trial registry (Deepakmb, 2011). This process is aimed at restoring transparency in research as medical journals are refusing to report any trial not registered before it is conducted in India. In 2004, the Indian regulatory framework launched the national pharmacovigilance system to support adverse drug reporting and as well as adoption and legalization of ICH-E6 GCP.

Public involvement in research and increasing push for the registration of ethic committees is seen as one of the influences of continued clinical research outsourcing. The Indian government has now mandated the registration of ethic committees as a pre-requisite for reviewing trials, delegated DCGI to enforce and determine the compensation that will be paid to research subjects in the event of death, injury, ADR, permanent disability or as incentive (Clinical trial ethics in Indian one step forward two steps backwards; The Tribune, February 23, 2013). These are in tandem with Western operations however the challenge remains with implementation and instituting punitive measures.

China recorded the first commercial gene therapy approval for cancer across the globe (Faiz & Eric, 2007). As controversial as gene therapy research, its approval in China demonstrates a level of trust in its research ethic conducts. However, about 250 million Chinese populations are partially insured while 800 million people remain uninsured. These people require quality medicine for their health and are willing to participate in clinical research either to gain access to life saving treatment or for monetary reasons. Thus the Chinese population remains vulnerable to research-related injuries and harm as their economic and health care needs demonstrate. (Drug development in China, opportunities and challenges a clinical trial perspective). This is in contrast to the Western world particularly the US where patients have options to treatment, and a well regulated ethical body.

Before 1985, research conduct was not completely coordinated. This was because the existing centralized drug regulatory process was not in place. In fact, ethic committees were lacking in some regions, there was no formal approval of research protocol before the conduct of trials. They also were not well informed about the research nor do they sign the informed consent forms (Jie Siu 2003). This, however, changed with the finalization and approval of GCP documents. This was also strengthened following the institution of the new drug law that required only ethically approval research to be conducted, certified clinical trial sites to conduct research; and trained and experienced principal investigators in GCP to conduct research.

Evolution of Indian ICH-GCP and the Chinese ICH-GCP processes

ICH is the International Conference on Harmonization of Technical Requirement for Registration of Pharmaceutical for human use.

As clinical research continued to expand across the major markets of Japan, the US, and Europe, the need to harmonize and have a common standard that will facilitate the acceptance of medicine researched in other countries became necessary. The ICH was formed to ensure that member countries comply with these sets of guidelines that cut across safety, efficacy, quality and multidisciplinary (cross cutting). Good Clinical Practice (GCP) is an international ethical and scientific quality standard for the design, conduct, performance, recording, analyses, reporting and publication of research involving human subject participation (International Conference on Harmonization). GCP is a subcomponent of the efficacy guideline that has its ethical principles consistent with the Helsinki declaration of 1964 and Belmont report of 1979. GCP has 13 core components that reflect ethical standards for the conduct of research. It was finalized and became operational in 1996 and 1997 respectively. However not many countries recognized it until the 2004 European Union clinical trial directive which revolutionized the use of the document as legal and enforced by law in the conduct of clinical trials(Carrying out clinical trial in India). Compliance to these standards provides assurance that the rights, welfare and protection of human subjects are guaranteed. In addition, it also assures the public that the data generated from the research are of high quality. This document is a fall out of reported research related harm, injuries, disability and death.

India's government and drug regulatory bodies- Central Drug Standard Control Organization (CDSCO), Indian Counsel of Medical Research (ICMR), Drug Technical Advisory

Committee (DTAC), and Drug Controller General Indian (DCGI) etcetera have all adopted guidelines in line with global regulatory framework.

The Indian counsel of Medical research first published its guidelines on research involving human subjects in 2000 (carrying out clinical trial in India; ethical concerns in clinical trial in Indian: an Investigation). These guidelines essentially reflected ICH-GCP, WHO guidelines and declaration of Helsinki. The guideline was reviewed in 2006 and persistently awaiting approval for implementation. Faced with the challenges of creating a balance between ethics and trade following the increasing outsourcing of clinical trials, the Drug Technical Advisory committee endorsed the adoption of GCP into Schedule Y which is the regulation that governs clinical trial legislative in the country (Carrying out clinical trial in India).

Before 2005, the drug and cosmetic rule under schedule Y suggest but did not require ethic review of submitted clinical trial document. This is one core component of the ICH-E6GCP guideline- which reads 'All trials before it is conducted must receive a favorable opinion/approval of a competent ethic committee or institutional review board'. However, effective January, 2005 it was required that all clinical trial reports clearly state that the trial was conducted according to ethical principles as declared by Helsinki, Indian GCP and ICMR ethical guidelines for biomedical research on human (Ethical concerns in clinical trial in Indian). This clearly shows the increasing recognition of GCP by Indian regulation and efforts to make its regulatory framework at par with global clinical trial demand. The question remains how equivalent is Indian GCP with ICH-E6GCP? And what punitive measures are in place to punish offenders as clearly stated in the European 2004 clinical trial declarative on adherence to GCP?

The Chinese GCP was finalized in 1995 and formally put into law in 1999. The newly formed China State Food and Drug Administration enforced GCP (sFDA) through the new drug law in 2001.

sFDA also ensures the certification of clinical trial sites in China in compliance with China GCP. This clearly shows China's regulatory control edge over Indian in the application of GCP.

The Chinese drug regulatory system upholds GCP practices such that only GCP certified public institutions are allowed to conduct clinical trials. GCP became recognized in China in the 1990s through international academic communications and exchanges as well as multinational pharmaceutical investment in China (Good Clinical Practice-compliant clinical practice in China). The increasing globalization of clinical trials, strategic alliances of companies, single ownership enterprise, and international CRO have driven the process of international standards in clinical research practices in China (Good Clinical Practice-compliant clinical practice in China). This act has prospered GCP practice in China.

However despite the recognized differences in the Chinese GCP and the ICH E6-GCP document, the standard of Chinese GCP is the same with the ICH-E6GCP document (Good Clinical Practice-compliant clinical practice in China). The challenges remain whether these differences further provide protection for subjects of research, or if these differences are part of the regulatory complexities multinational companies continue to encounters while conducting clinical trials in China?

Intellectual property protection, government role and involvement in research

The introduction of pharmaceutical product patent in 2005 has stimulated research and development (R&D) activities in India pharmaceutical sector. This also addressed public health needs as quality medicines were accessed by the public (India and the drug patent war). However lack of understanding of this law may mar the projected gains envisaged from intellectual property rights.

Before 2005, Indian law allowed only process patent which has little protection on intellectual property right for companies promoting research and development in the country. This gap created a flourish of copying and reverse engineering among Indian companies producing medicines locally. Furthermore, this has strengthened the generic capacity and capability of Indian pharmaceutical companies in providing low price drugs of varying quality in the Indian market (India and the drug patent war). The flip side to this is that true research and development continued to suffers including access to quality medicines. In 2005, the Indian government extended its World Trade Organization Trade related intellectual property rights (WTO-TRIPS) to include pharmaceutical products. This initiative is meant to revamp the country's pharmaceutical companies to focus more on R&D as against the generic dominated home front with attendant gains of patent protection. In addition this is also an incentive for multinational companies who hold patents to medicine important to Indian health care need (India and the drug patent war).

However, this dream appears to be a mirage as certain clause that are not in tandem with the WTO TRIPS agreement are found within the Indian patent law. The clause which reads "the derivative of known substances cannot be patented unless it demonstrates differences in terms of efficacy' (India and the drug patent war). This remains a big hurdle for the multinational companies to cross and indeed may serves as drawback to true R&D in the country.

The question is who determines the satisfactory level of efficacy in this case? There are two stand point to this debate- the clause came into be as many companies perpetrated variants of existing drugs which the Indian government referred to as frivolous innovation- in the American parlance me too drugs. Novartis a multinational company lost a case on glivec a more stable form of gleevec due to this clause. The other view is that Indian patent hurdle discourages multinational from supporting R&D unique to Indian health needs as this clause provides freedom for continual multiplication of generic variants of patented medicines in other regulated markets. This is a revelation following clinical trial outsourcing to Indian pharmaceutical market.

Government involvement and role in research in Indian is replete with innovations to enhance Indian pharmaceutical market in several ways. These include though not limited to: 1) the Indian government in support of R&D had issued guidelines since 2001 through the Indian Drug Policy Control Order for tax exemptions for 10 years for innovative new drugs developed in India, 2) 2005 adoption and implantation of GCP with guidelines consistent with declaration of Helsinki, 3) Indian government engagement in multinational trials-Parallel phase II and III studies can now be commenced at par with other countries, 4) the government made interesting amendments in her drug and cosmetic rule in tandem with global regulatory framework published in February 2013(Mandatory registration of clinical trials ethical approval of all trials etcetera).

Intellectual property right move started much earlier in the Chinese system compared with the Indian pharmaceutical sector (The effect of changing intellectual property on pharmaceutical industry in Indian and China). The move towards intellectual property protection started in 1993 with Chinese reform of her patent law. Introduction of the WTO-TRIPS agreement into its framework took effect in 2002 with further extension of its patent law to 20 years including extension of data for exclusivity for 6 years. Market right exclusivity in India remain a challenge and unclear as only new molecules are granted such waiver (India and the drug patent war)

The WTO-TRIPs agreement in the Chinese system incorporated the pharmaceutical sector unlike the Indian government that allowed pharmaceutical inclusion in 2005. Patent right filing is handled by the Chinese State Intellectual Property Office (SIPO). The filing system which is the – "The first filing system" is in tandem with the rest of the world as against the US which follows the first inventor rule (China's current IPR environment). Even with well-established statutory structure to guide intellectual property protection, clinical study outsourcing showed that China is not different from Indian as over 20% of products are counterfeit and pirated (China's current IPR environment). Significant effort has also being made by the central government to curb these excesses however measures put in place still remain weak.

Indian and Chinese economic reality in drug development

As companies move their businesses to emerging markets, they stand the chance of enjoying reduced operational costs across the different aspects of clinical trials. Reduced cost is seen with professional fees, site fees, procedural fees, overhead or administrative fees.

However, as big pharma-industries reposition to capture these markets, the impact on the economy as a nation and the people of the country cannot be emphasized enough.

India's pharmaceutical market, according the associated chambers of commerce, was set to capture 1 - 2 billion global pharmaceutical capital market in 2010 (Clinical trial in India; Jankosky, Jiang, & Farwell, 2007). As of 2003, the Indian pharmaceutical market supported 3% of global trial while in 2010 this figure climbed to 10% and expected to rise by another 5% in 2011 (Jankosky, Jiang, & Farwell, 2007; Deepakmb, 2011). From 2000 to 2004, only 60-170 registered trials were conducted in India while in 2011 that number rose to 1,850. This is a rise in excess of almost 11 times in one year (2011) compared to a 4 year period in the past (2000-2004)(Jankosky, Jiang, & Farwell, 2007; Clinical trial ethics in India: one step forward and two steps backwards).

Phase I/II and III studies in the US cost about 20/50 and 100 million dollars respectively in the United States. This cost is halved when the study is moved to India and as well 75 times faster in conducting the studies (Deepakmb, 2011). The cost of professionals, overhead, and procedure fees is about 50%, 20%, and 21% lower compared to the American market respectively.

As intriguing as this appears to pharmaceutical companies carrying out their trade in India, the Indian economy shares a large proportion of this interest across its sectors. It is estimated that India has the highest number of FDA accredited laboratories across the globe-an increasing impact of global clinical trial outsourcing (Jankosky, Jiang, & Farwell, 2007).

It is also expected that these laboratories with their locations and the good road networking in India will support a greater number of these trial with attendant financial rewards .About 80 thousand hospitals in Indian are currently engaged in clinical trial. These hospitals would require infrastructural development either in kind or in cash from the sponsor pharmaceuticals which also contribute to access to quality care and economic revamping of such hospital in supporting service delivery. In addition, these facilities would require more trained professional in the clinical research field thus creating employment for a critical mass in the country. It was projected in 2011 that Indian will need about 50,000 clinical research professionals to meet the clinical trial boom in the country (Statistical Review of Clinical Research Industry). India's population stand at an advantage of lower drug pricing as the developed medicines enter the Indian market (Deepakmb, 2011). Furthermore, local capacity is built from constant interaction with international influx. The capacity building is seen with training of investigators and other clinical research professionals in ethics, as well as indigenous CRO. Finally, India is projected to begin clinical trial outsourcing between 2013 and 2015(Statistical Review of Clinical Research Industry).

The Chinese market cannot be left out with over 800 million and 250 million uninsured and partially insured population respectively coupled with abundance of disease resource. The Chinese market was projected to be the 5th largest market in 2010 and would become the third largest in 2020 (Jankosky, Jiang, & Farwell, 2007). Growth of clinical trial sprang from 4% in 2007 to 10% in 2010(Jankosky, Jiang,& Farwell, 2007).

China is second to India when its clinical trial growth rate is compared with Singapore, Pakistan, and Sri Lanka over 2002-2008(Statistical Review of Clinical Research Industry).However, China has better prospects when it comes to attractiveness as it lags behind the US by 2.78% while leading India with 0.52% (Statistical Review of Clinical Research Industry) The number of global multinational multicenter trial in China is increasing by the day. There are nine reported international multicenter trials sponsored by AstraZeneca involving 130 domestic hospitals in China. China is currently featured in the GLOBE phase III hepatitis B trial hosted in 20 countries -the first of its kind across the globe- with China contributing 25% of the subject (Faiz & Eric, 2007). China also successfully recorded the first cancer gene treatment clinical trials in the world. (Faiz & Eric, 2007).

Despite its bureaucratic challenges culminating to lengthy approval processes, large pharmaceutical companies including biotechnology companies find its economic reality fascinating. Phase I and II clinical trials cost about 15-20% of what it takes to conduct studies in the United States. The growth rate of local CRO, their adherence to ICH-GCP and their ability to monitor and oversee trials are fascinating. Exposure to international trials and protocols, strategic alliances and collaboration with international CRO makes the Chinese market interesting.

In 2005 30% of the 400 clinical trials reported where facilitated by CRO (Faiz & Eric, 2007).There is an increasing wave of building offices and research infrastructures by large pharmaceuticals including international CROs owing structures in China. This is in support of their global repositioning and enhancement of their network of global and local trials in China.

However, the Chinese economy is also poised to ensure that profiteering of pharmaceutical industries is distributed across board. One such approach is the restriction of sample export for further analysis thus facilitating domiciliation of financial rewards in the laboratory sectors. Chinese institutions are collaborating with their foreign counterparts to domicile clinical research and ethics training in China (Emerging Markets). Local CRO growth in number, capacity and capabilities is another form of promoting local content in the Chinese economy. With Chinese current attractiveness for clinical research and US continual increase in funding clinical trials (over 31 billion dollars spent in 2011), the economic reality and impact remain to be imagined.

Conclusions

The clinical trial enterprise is one that evolves every day and needs to keep pace with emerging issues across the globe as the people; practice and countries are at different levels of operation when it comes to clinical research conduct. Moving clinical research beyond the big 3 of US, Europe and Japan to other countries particularly to economies with potentials and evolving research structures focused on meeting global clinical study will require expertise.

These expertise are needed to capture subtle changes and enabling environments these economies present when included either in multinational studies or when studies are conducted in-country for optimum benefit.

While legal, regulatory and ethical structures in India and China continue to grow to meet international standards, there is need for multinational companies (MNC) to demonstrate best practices and quality enhancement system- which may be lacking in these regions for effective research conduct. The health care administration, structure and level of development make the population of these countries over-dependent on research for cure, access to quality treatment, and sometimes for money.

Legal, regulatory and ethical requirements must be consciously sought by both parties (MNCs and research structures in India and China) before, during and while closing out a trial in these countries. As cost reduction, time to complete trials, available human subjects including pressure to meet medical needs drive the research vehicle to Indian and China, focus must not be lost on the requirements of qualification, experience, and training needs of professionals in these countries before engagement in research.

The big 3- US, Europe and Japan including observer countries (Canada and Australia) which saw the need to harmonize research practices including accommodating data extrapolation, constituted the ICH with revisions to match evolving practices in research conduct. As a fallout of research misconduct, several documents including Helsinki Declaration and Belmont Report were put together to respond to human subject protection in the conduct of research (ICH-GCP).

As Industries and Regulatory bodies from lead pharmaceutical markets influenced the ICH program, they still remain relevant in calling for a wider stakeholder involvement using the same ICH vehicle as clinical trials capitalization move to potential regions. This is because lead pharma-industries from these 3 countries, continue to expand to these new market while drawing profit from the market strengths (low cost, abundant disease resource, large number of treatment naïve patients, abundant and low work force, high retention clinical trial rate, weak regulatory and ethical structures) and yet complain of the difficulties encountered in conducting clinical trials in India and China.

Unmasking grey areas of global clinical trials remain an avenue of moving research forward as a living science and meeting human needs. Access to life saving medicines remains a mirage to poor populations who contributed to the development of these medicines. The huge market developers (Pharmaceutical industries) stand to enjoy should they foster balance in availability, access, and pricing. On the other hand, harmonizing intellectual property protection for pharmaceutical products require attention as this will encourage research relevant to population thus addressing issues with access to life saving medicines and genetic diversity in humans (sub-populations).

As language barriers present obstacle in Indian and China, strategic alliance and collaboration must be seen as effort towards improving the free flow of research rather than increasing cost. China is setting the pace in this direction as regulatory bodies require most operation to be guided by local partners. This should produce healthy relationship rather than serve as obstacles to research.

Finally, what does the future hold with the stringent regulation and monitoring of research? How will the more informed human subjects who know their rights react when engaged in research in emerging markets? The effect is far researching and will be determined by global regulation of research conduct.

References

China's Clinical Trial Boom - Language Connectionswww.languageconnections.com/.../China's%20Clinical%20Trial%20Boom.pdf

EMERGING MARKETS: NAVIGATING THE PATH TO CONDUCTSUCCESSFUL...
www.medpace.com/PDF/ConductingTrialsInChina.pdf · PDF file

Opportunities and challenges for clinical research in India ...pharma.financialexpress.com/20051215/ipcspecial05.shtml

Doing Anything for the Cure: Exploitation through the Globalization ...nchchonors.org/wp.../2012/.../Bedera-Nicole-Westminster-College-Paper.pdf –

Phillips, C. J. (2005). Health economics: An introduction for health professionals. Malden, MA: Blackwell Publishing.

Dr.Surinder Singh
Clinical Trials New Horizon India. pharmexcil.com/data/uploads/clinicaltrials.dr.surinder.ppt · PPT

Clinical trials in India: ethical concerns www.who.int/bulletin/volumes/86/8/08-010808.pdf · PDF file 2008

Practical Aspects India of Conducting Clinical Trials 1,2 in India
www.amarexcro.com/articles/docs/RAPS_Focus_Practical_Feb2009.pdf · PDF file 2009

Deepakmb. (2011). Clinical Trial Regulation In India

www.legalservicesindia.com/article/article/clinical-trial...

Clinical trial ethics in India: One step forward, two steps back

www.ncbi.nlm.nih.gov › ... › v.3(2); Apr-Jun 2012

Patient Protection in Clinical Trials in India: Some Concerns www.ncbi.nlm.nih.gov › ... 2010

How to Conduct Clinical Trials in China.

https://www.leaddiscovery.co.uk/reports/1306/How_to_Conduct...

Faiz Kermani, Eric Langer (2007) . Clinical Trials In China - BioPlan Associates

www.bioplanassociates.com/.../ContrPharma_ClinTrialsChina_May07.pdf · PDF file

BMTA Clinical Trials Globalization Nov2008.ppt

www.bmtadvisors.com/docs/Globalization%20of%20Clinical%20Trials.pdf · PDF file

Jurij Petrin. Regulatory Implications of Global Clinical Trials

prs-clinical.com/documents/Global%20Clinical%20Trial%20-%20... · PDF file

PPT – Drug Development in China: Opportunities and Challenges ...

www.powershow.com/view/399aa-ODdmZ/Drug_Development_in_China...

Carrying out Clinical Trials in India - ECRON ACUNOVA

www.acunovalife.com/pdf/whitepapers/RAJ_Pharma%20June%202010... · PDF file

Ethical concerns in clinical trials in India: an investigation

www.fairdrugs.org/uploads/files/Ethical_concerns_in_clinical... · PDF file

India and the Drug Patent Wars - Health - AEI

www.aei.org/article/health/india-and-the-drug-patent-wars

The Effect of Changing Intellectual Property on Pharmaceutical ...

www.who.int/hiv/amds/Grace2China.pdf · PDF file

Mukesh Kumar PhD RAC (2009). Practical Aspects of conducting clinical trials in India. Retrieved from www.amarexcro.com/articles/.../RAPS_Focus_Practical_Feb2009.pdfFile Format: PDF/Adobe Acrobat - Quick View

Chatterjee, P. (2008). Clinical trials in India: Ethical concerns. Bulletin of the World Health Organization, 86(8), 581–582. Retrieved from http://ezp.waldenulibrary.org/login?url=http://search.ebscohost.com/login.aspx?direct=true&db=a9h&AN=33717667&site=ehost-live&scope=site 3

Jankosky, J., Jiang, Y., & Farwell, T. (2007). Grant budgeting and negotiating in India and China. Applied Clinical Trials, 16(11), 56–62. Retrieved from http://ezp.waldenulibrary.org/login?url=http://search.ebscohost.com/login.aspx?direct=true&db=a9h&AN=27459305&site=ehost-live&scope=site 4

Li Jinju. Regulation and Views on Drug Clinical Trials in China www.apec-ahc.org/files/tp201002/Session4_LiJinJu.pdf · PDF file

Protecting Your Intellectual Property Rights in China

mac.doc.gov/China/Docs/BusinessGuides/IntellectualPropertyRights.htm

Geetanjali Parab, Priyanka Mudllar, Shvangi Patil, Srabani Biwas, Tanmay Shinde, Class Pgdaib. Statistical Review of Clinical Research Industry. Retrieved from www.slideshare.net

HigHligHts - WIPO - World Intellectual Property Organization
www.wipo.int/export/sites/www/ipstats/en/wipi/pdf/941_2012... · PDF file

The Tribune, February 23, 2013.Clinical trials claimed 436 live in 2012, online edition